Dancing
with the Divine

Dancing
with the Divine

Michael Murphy Burke

MOUNTAIN ARBOR
PRESS

Mountain Arbor
Press
Alpharetta, GA

ISBN: 978-1-63183-090-7

10 9 8 7 6 5 4 3 2   0 3 0 6 1 7

Printed in the United States of America

♾This paper meets the requirements of ANSI/NISO Z39.48-1992 (Permanence of Paper)

*"Yesterday I was clever,
so I wanted to change the world.
Today I am wise, so I am changing myself."*
—Rumi

Contents

Foreword

It is my pleasure to introduce you to Michael Burke and to the tapestry of language, passion, and deep insight that awaits you on the following pages. I have known Michael for many years and have always been mesmerized by the wisdom and beauty that flows from his heart and his pen. The scope of this man's creativity is immense, ranging from the profoundly spiritual to the utterly earthy. No matter the subject matter, what streams from this man's mind is genuinely inspiring. When reading Michael Burke's poetry one can expect tears of ecstasy, whimsical delights, intellectual and sensual stirrings, and the answers to deep inner longings. His talent to marry the deeply esoteric with the raw human experience is the sign of a true mystic whose verses are as relevant and sacred as any ancient scripture.

Michael invites his readers into a dance of imagination that leaves endless space for co-creation. So as you enter this collection, be fully prepared to partner with him in the spaces between the verses, the void between the stanzas, and the spiritual invitations between each word. His unique ability to stir his reader's soul is profound, and each new reading will provide undiscovered revelations. Be prepared, this lover of language will awaken much within you. His is a voice that must be heard, a heart that must be experienced, and a wisdom that must be known.

Each poem that Michael shares is a mystical journey rampant with rich and unfettered imagery. Each offering has so many dimensions to it that one must truly stop and savor the multiple layers contained within each line before moving to the next. No word is there by accident. Each one has been carefully chosen to cultivate a plethora of textures and meanings. This is the mark of a true craftsman. Michael Burke is a sincere artist who knows that no word should be wasted and no idea made insignificant. Each one is a precious gift and is delivered with the greatest of respect for the language, the reader, and the Divine Source from whence they come.

As a minister I spend a great deal of time searching for ways to convey meaning and significance to the lives of those whom I serve. It is my job to transport a congregation from the mundane to the extraordinary. To do so, I must first make the journey myself. I have at my disposal the typical inspiration found in the words of great prophets to aid me, but as many times as not, it is my contemporaries that help me find the path. I consider Michael to be a lay minister at the top of that list. I find in his works the catalyst for deeper insight and the spark of an awakened fire. It is no accident that I invite Michael to share his poetry in person at our services. The success of the message is almost assured when there is such lavish ground on which to build. In addition, he delivers his poems with a bass voice so succulent that it melts the hardened human exterior almost immediately.

Let me digress for a moment from Michael Burke's words and reflect upon the nature of the man. Behind the flowery language is a man undeniably full of love and a seeker who yearns for humanity's awakening. This poetry is much more than Michael's art; it is his mission. There is a clarity of purpose that transcends his words and belies a true desire to raise the collective vibration. This noble cause will not be hidden in the text, but will be evident as the very source of each rhyme, rhythm, and reflection. Feel it, hear it, and unite in his vision as you read. I honor Michael's quest and the numerous ways it is playing out in the manifest realm. I honor him for his humble, unassuming presence that appears to be unaware of the difference he makes on the planet and in the lives of individuals. He is a sincere servant of the Divine, and I honor him for the myriad of ways that he demonstrates, teaches, and lives his poetic message of love.

I wish you, the reader, all the exquisite goodness that I have received from Michael's poetry and heart, as I challenge you to drink deeply and often from this invaluable volume of spiritual treasures.

—Rev. Richard Burdick

Acknowledgments

I acknowledge that there is truly no way to thank all the various energies that have inspired and awakened the shaping of my evolution.

All the idiosyncrasies and serendipities that have come into word are the poems you shall read on these pages—and only the Divine can possibly know the "audiosyncrasies" that will awaken in listening to the audiobook.

From my first breath of inspiration as I wrote about being born, I have been born again and again with each poem. I have found inspiration EVERY-WHERE!

From before my incredible early English teachers, Mrs. Patrick and Mrs. Westbrook, to the elusive muses of Now . . . I say thank you.

I thank Candace Apple for providing a place for poets to perform and share.

I thank Unity North and Richard Burdick for their immaculate commitment to freedom of expression.

I thank my mother and father for my birth into this consciousness.

I thank my Grandfather B and my Grandmother T for gifts beyond words.

I thank my children for imparting love into my every breath.

I thank every scrap of wood and paper that I have ever written down a thought upon.

I thank my cousin, Lorna, for my first beautifully bound writing book. It not only brought a new passion to my writing (see "Deep Inside of You," pg. 98), it brought a new respect.

I honor my years at The Poets Studio with Walter Griffin and all the other poets.

I learn from everyone!

And I am honored now to share my poems as a way of saying "thank you."

Thank you to the Divine dancing with us ALL!

—Michael Murphy Burke, 2016

Peace

The Echo of Light

I only know one way to shine
So I shine ever so bright
I am the vibration of sound
Yes, I am the Echo of Light

I am borne in the breath of beginning
And I bathe in stillness that's spinning
I can be nowhere else
And nowhere else can be me

I am image and reflection
I am death and resurrection
I am the age that I am
Because of the age of the plan

I am not a moment too soon
I am the Earth, the Sun, and the Moon
I am less a constellation
And more its creation

I am the moment that's expressed
I am the bless in all that's blessed
I am the touch of God's finger
I am the moment of linger
I am neither yet or before
Neither water nor shore

For in the Almighty's eye
I am not even I

I am the truth of a miracle
I am fluid and lyrical
I am the song I am to be
Through the Art of Harmony

Know that Grace is the sound
And Christ is the key
I lock into worship and worship frees me to see
That I am the moment before the moment is me

And I shine
Yes I shine
Ever so bright
I am the sound of sight
Yes, I am the Echo of Light.

Saturation

Spirit told me to lay down on Mother Earth
at the Etowah Indian Mounds
So I did
And I began to hear
at first
little sounds
that gently became this delicate conversation
between each blade of grass
They were dancing with mycelium
The earth's internet
The Windows of roots
So that all can see into one another
No separation
Just saturation
A connection so complete
that it is not a connection
It is One
One elaborate conversation
between One eternal existence
and Itself

The vision we see with our eyes
Eyes that are made of millions of atoms
that were formed in the stars
that they are now witness to
Evolutionary irony
Creation's vision of its own Creation
And in that vision am I
Which from Spirit's point of view is
I am
Which,
when I eventually,
finely tuned in,
was what each blade of grass was actually saying
to each other
In Union
I Am
I Am
Yet I heard them separate at first
They never were
I was
Now
I am NOT.

Divine Expression

Am I not the shell cracking open
for the seed to sprout
As well as the growth that comes
from within to without

Am I not the Light
that provides the nutrients
As well as the Source
within all its filaments

Am I not all of the elements
And all of their impermanence

Am I not the changing
as well as the change
Am I not the home
no matter where the range

Am I not the wandering itself
As well as the wanderer
For in my travels to myself
I find I am Him
as well as Her

I am whole
as well as each session

I am the balance
of Divine expression.

Aspiring

In the life of a tree
There exists a root
That digs deeper than any other
There exists a branch
That reaches higher than any other
There exists a leaf
That flutters
And fetches the wind
More gracefully than any other

Yet these individuals are part of the whole
They are held up to the light
And dug deeper in the darkness
By those who assist them
Some are watered, some are parched
Some are frozen, some are thawed
Some are on fire and some are burned up
All are something that is evolving

Into something else
Their very life is supported
By the death of others.

They eat of the earth they create
They breathe of the air
That surrounds and abounds
With memories of futures passed
And volumes of mythical elegance
That cross vast vineyards
And mountainous meanderings
To reach into each other
And release the essence of one another
Offering the taste of resilience
Baring the scent of communion
For all to breathe
Deep in their roots
And high in their branches

We are all leaves on this tree of life
And all our thoughts
Are what waters our growth
From scattered saplings
To full-fledged forests
We are the nutritional supply
That nourishes our next
As well as the delirious demand
that desires our now

We come and go with each breath

It is when we think we are falling
That we are actually flying
It is when we experience dying in our life
That we actually experience life in our dying
For it is in our disassembly
As structures and systems
That we assemble ourselves
Into pure existence
What often appears in our perception
As a step back
Is more often a universal aspiration
To move ahead

Every move is an act of God

We are digging our roots deeper
And reaching our branches higher
At all times

Because there is no reverse.

The Thought of God

When you realize that you
Are an expression of God
It is easy for you
To express that God

Easy's not simple
Simple takes practice
Practice becomes ritual
Ritual becomes easy

It is in our blood
It is in our bones
It is in our cells

Gratitude breeds altitude
And as we learn to fly
Our wings teach us worship
For we are not only meant to worship
Worship is what we are meant to be

For it is not in the act of worship that I exist
I exist because I am the act of worship
Worship is Praise of Faith unseen
Worship is Love beyond thought

I know God
In everlasting Glory
Thought about me
And thus I became
The Thought of God.

To See

Waves of anger take a piece
Of every shore they leave
Little grains of our souls
Drowning their own reprieve

Swimming to no avail
Other breezes on our sail
Going along on someone else's ride
Is like trying to swim against the tide

Sounds impossible
But it's quite probable

Imagining we are in control
I mean, our hands are on the wheel
But the column is not connected to anything
It's there just for the feel

We grab it with an anguished relief
As if we were guiding the course
Hard to navigate around submerged islands
That shimmer under waves of remorse

Miracles exist in antiquated apothecaries
Where wizards weave spells from scepters
That grow from their heads like unicorns' horns
A point of entry housing mysterious receptors

Are we not mystical
Filled with the art of breathing
A species so full of mystery
That we conceive our own conceiving

We wonder more about where we come from
Than about where we are
A healthy dose of bewilderment
Seems a prerequisite so far

For bewilderment
lives next door to enlightenment

It gives us the what is
from what can be
We are the waves upon our own shore
Washing away ourselves
to See.

Reins

When intimacy exists within a program of pain
Then the overwhelming response is one of disdain
And though the program is not ours in creation
It is ours to deal with in this situation
In this particular cycle of being born
Which brought us into human form

And with that comes a history of synapses
Conditioned behaviors where our will collapses
For it knows not its own condition
It functions on an inherited tradition
One that galloped through our ancestors' brains
We're given the horses, but not the reins

We exist unaware of our subconscious rule
As if the castle moat were a swimming pool
Sometimes we would rather live with the devil
We know
Than to unearth the angel buried in our foe
Our inhabited behavior is our Ichabod
For by facing our demons, we find our God

Our past can be changed, we must claim these powers
Our DNA rearranged, our choices are ours
We must forgive ourselves, we must forgive our tribe
For their sins are elixirs, we need not imbibe
We shall drink of the life which we create
And love in each breath will be our fate

A future that gives us a perfect Now
And Faith in our Grace is how.

Within Our Service

Formed in the fire of birth
Cooled by the spinning earth

Colored by the breath of angels
As they paint me into being

I am mountain to the stream
I am all that's in between

The word and the sentence
The exodus of repentance

I am found in your cells
And lost in the bells
That echo Christ
As He laughed out loud
Undraped our sins upon a shroud
That speaks to us today

In an esoteric way
To say without delay
That we are here to play
Up until the very last
The role in which we're cast

Know thyself and know thy purpose
Our reward exists within our service.

The Elixir of an Answer

Do you know there is Christ in every move you make
Do you know there is Buddha in every breath you take
Do you know there are hands that help you
Long before you ever reach out
Do you take account that there is no moment
You are alone

It is very difficult to notice God
Every second of every minute of every day
But
She is always there
And so is He
The Divine Union
is One

Do you notice God in between
The colors of a rainbow
Do you notice God

In the crown of sunshine
Or the halo of rain
On any given day
Do you know you are always arriving
At a home you never left

Or do you hibernate within a reality
Laced with illusion
A disturbed delusion

A life half full
In a universe overflowing

Drinking the wine of what, when, how, and why
But only ever swallowing
The elixir of an answer

For these are of no concern
To the coming of light
For it has already arrived
Always been
Ever will be

We are but wicks
Sealed inside a colored wax of clay
Melting our past to reshape our future
When we can only burn NOW
So, why wait

Burn Bright
FLOW

Feed the seed
Of your own evolution
Be the leader
Of your own revolution

We are only separate
As long as we see someone else

The truth is
We Are All Light
And that's All Right.

When Your Wisdom
Reaches Its Will

I stumbled on your purity
And have known of nothing since
That can quite encapsulate
Your bewildered recompense

Your beauty lies befuddled
By the doubts you hold so true
Let the past be just a memory
The future waits for you

With open arms that lay in want
Of all that you can be
I am here to tell you
Self-doubt need not be

You are wise beyond your years
You are blessed for just to be
And when your aura finds you
You will shine for all to see

You are radiant in your hiding
Like a blind that doesn't close
Just a glimpse is all I've seen
And that's enough to predispose

That I might have fucked up
By not leaving long ago
I think I oversaturated the soil
In which your flower tried to grow

By wanting so hard to help
I may have condemned the commitment
Sometimes it is not my place
To further the course of contentment

One of the hardest things for me to do
Is to let go
Breathe free of the people
That I believe need me so

Why do I feel such an urge
To help another
Why sometimes does my help
Serve to smother

The powers that could be
If I would just step away
Let them be their own savior
Seed the blossoms of decay

Separate roots need different wells
To satiate their thirst
I have come to see that second
Is a bridge to being first

What is not said is golden
In between the spoken word
And right is of no consequence
If it borders on absurd

For each and every one of us
Is uniquely suited to
The teachings of a teacher
That are only meant for you

So to disregard their brilliance
And disturb the evenflow
Is to disrespect their purpose
And postpone what all must know

I must leave, I must not
I am here until I'm gone
I will infiltrate the darkness
Till your mind reflects the dawn

The pot has reached its boil
May your eyes begin to see
Release your troubled memories
And the peace of you will be

You are destined for the karma
That shall turn your inside out
And together we will separate
Your self from your self-doubt.

Crawling in Silk

When I listen to the water
I can taste the music
The thundering silence of depth
Arises in my dolphins

I am a reflection of that
Which shines the shadows
A seed of light planted in darkness
Awaits my awakening

The time has come
For wolf to become phoenix
No longer shall I sleep
In sheep's clothing

It is the third trimester
In the birth of a butterfly
And the infusion of transition has begun

I am about to fly once more
Before I land in another life
To begin again the crawl
That must precede the walk
That is vital to the leap
Which begins my flight again.

One Can Only

I obtain my faith
By having my questions answered
Yet I sustain my faith
By having my answers questioned
I am within the Will of God
When I am without the want
For such a Deity
In seeking for anything
Outside of me
I awaken the energy
Inside of me
It is this energy
That enables me to search
It is this energy
That lay in the shadow
From the Light of Energy

I cannot think of not thinking
Of something
Without thinking of it
This is the essence of duality
When I release the essence of thinking
I become thought itself
The only expression of God
That there is

A unified singularity

A Divinity divided is not less Divine
It is diminished in power
It is a fractal Deity
It becomes a segmented secularism
And it turns on itself
To gain the advantage
Of unified power
When, actually, in this case

To surrender is to conquer

No power equal to itself
Can defeat itself

It must realize
Defeat is but annihilation
Of some of its own power

This illusion is disillusioned
By the acceptance of surrender

The veil cannot hide One

It can only conceal
One from the Other

When the separation is severed
And Union is seen as

Never Being Separate

The veil is no more

And I exist as One
Only One
I inhale only God
I exhale only God
I speak of nothing
No Thing
Because I am only One
I have no thing to speak of
Because there is nothing
Outside of me

Any expression I can express
Is an expression of the One

Therefore Now and Forever More
The penultimate statement
Of all time
Will never change

The only real Truth
There is
Is the Divine statement
I Am That I Am

For One cannot know God
One can only Be God.

Web of Wonder

I heard the wind whistle
Through the webs of wonder
Woven by the spirits of serenity
For just that purpose
To bring outer sound
To inner silence

To capture the breath
Of the Beloved
In Sacred reverberation
And release the blessing
Of the Grace within

I saw crystals dancing
On these strings of infinite patterns
Glistening in the vibration of love
Pulsing with perfection
Singing with the saints

Aligned with angels
Whose tears of joy they represent
By sprinkling free from captured essence
To splash upon disciples
As they become apostles

Rooted in the earth
Yet blossoming in Heaven
Captured in their time
Yet beyond that constraint

A vision of the future
Is a look into the past
For where we are going
Is where we came from

And woven in that
Web of wonder
Is all of us
Before we were
Any of us.

Sense Less;
Sense More

When we stop searching for meaning
We start to discover miracles
The very essence of our sixth sense
Is to go beyond our five senses
We see, smell, taste, hear, and feel

But our sense
Our Unknowing Knowing

The tap on our shoulders
That touches our wings

The whisper of winds
That speak beyond tongues

The taste of what is
In the thought of another

The smell of memory
In the breath of love

The touch of a Christ
Through the eyes in a mirror

These are the subtle
Sub-modalities

The way the strings
Of our cells
Sing the sounds
Of our names

A practiced perfection
That is the perfect practice

It is exquisite entrainment
For the sense beyond sense

Learn to stop searching
For meaning
And begin to discover
Miracles.

Aquatic Angels

Long ago, long before we inhabited this planet
Angels swam with dolphins and left their mark

More precisely
Their cosmic energy
Within
These aquatic angels
These submerged saints
Our rare brothers and sisters
These diving disciples
Mammals who live in the water
These acrobatic avatars
Are our ancient ancestors

Blessed with a connection to Spirit
That echoes in the sound of their singing

What's perceptible is life changing
What's imperceptible has already changed us
These are the frequencies of our fundamentals

And their arc when they swim
An expression of Grace
Is the same as the magnetic arc
Around this very planet

As they play they infuse our Earth
With wisdom energy
So we may walk
As dolphins of the land
Allowing our arcs to caress
The air in which we swim

Let us give to that air
What they give to the water

For when you come with Love
Love will come to you.

Interiority Complex

Demons brought to light
Are angels set on fire
I day the night
With blind desire
For that I've yet to see

Has seen me

It cannot be
If it's free

Free of the cage
I built to engage
Its sorry views
And mortal blues
Its endless defenses
And infinite fences
Its drudge to begrudge

And bind my mind
Its urge to splurge
And tie my high

On low vibrations
Insincere sensations

It wants me crippled
Dependent and nippled
Feeding on the faults
It festers in my vaults
Cause it knows when its empty
I receive what is meant me

The love I sought in my life
Was seeking for me every day
But it took a vision of my ex-wife
For me to get out of the way
And then
Just as suddenly
My father appeared
Riding bareback on a giant eagle
His cosmic aura
Tangling with the solar winds
He looked so royal
He looked so regal

Then he raised his arms above his head
And before disappearing into the Light
I saw written on the back of his white leather jacket

Everything's gonna be alright

Then I appeared in the sky
All of it
There was nothing that wasn't me
And I found everything I'd been searching for
By finding nothing was outside of me

I was the beating of the eagle's heart
The resurrection of a widowed spirit
I am light to my own night
I am dawn to my own day
Because your love allowed me to fear it

And in that fear was release
And in that release was peace
And in that peace is peace within
And peace within is inner peace
And inner peace has always known

That Love knew what I was
Before I ever knew what Love was.

Six Strings of Spirit

He played a guitar strung
With six strings of spirit
And he strummed as if Grace
Were his fingers
Caressing each string
Like the wind on a rose
Each sound a fragrance
That lingers

I can hear the bouquet
Strong as café au lait
And the muse begins her call
As a song from the heart
That plays every part
Of the One within us all

The notes he plays
They bend in ways
That come from the Divine

He's the vessel that fills
The glass of our wills
We drink his music like wine

It serenades our cells
With the stories it tells
Ancient songs are born again
And though a word
Is never heard
Spirit sings from deep within

These strings of his
They must be spun
From the Hair of God
The Gifted One

For music is the way He speaks
And love is the way She sings
Play your guitar, my beautiful friend
For you flow from Nature's springs

And the mist you release
Gives inner peace
Each moment not a moment
Too soon
For we find our way
Every time you play
And get closer to being
In Tune.

See-Saw

What blessings appear for me to see
All come down to what I saw

Is perception a gift of recollection
Can Truth be seen by its own inception
Do I produce what I create
Or am I created by what I produce
Does a revelation actually reveal
Or am I revealed by the revelation
For in getting to know my Self
I must let go of myself
All that I know that's related to vision
Conjures upon me a state of division
The painting is done before I begin
But it's up to me how the colors come in
For to see is all about what I draw
From what it is I think I saw

Is a moment of Divine clarity
A clearer perception of this painted confusion
Do my mirrors somehow become windows
And are the windows part of the illusion
I don't have to see through to see within
But I must go within to see through
I believe the answer to Who Am I
Lies in the question Who Are You

Why did I draw you in to my life
And why did you draw me in yours
Is it to show that our happily ever afters
Are actually all happily ever befores

I'm a child on both sides of a seesaw
As one goes up the other goes down
And through a repeating point of balance
A constant comes around
And that is . . .
That I can truly trust
This child in my playground
Who knows that balance
Is not something searched for
Balance is something
Constantly found.

Balancing Light

The rays of morning
Dance through the trees
A ballet of dawning
Of possibilities

Each strand of light
A gift from above
To allow us insight
Into what we're made of

Darkness seems
To disappear
But is it gone
Or is it here
Is night a pillow
On which day may lay
Or a warm soft blanket
That wants day to stay

Does night disillusion
And fractal the facts
Or does night go within
And ask us to ask

What has it been that day has meant
And how well did we abuse it
Impermanence is permanent
Can't find it until you lose it

A gift not taken
Is a lesson learned
A talent unused
Is a blessing returned

We are given this balance
To help carry on
Because each day's night
Is another day's dawn

We sleep in dreams
That seem a place
That's out of time
But full of space

We seek in slumber
Like children at play

And soak in the night
To balance the day

So dawn, sweet Dawn
And shine my Soul
Then bring me the Night
So I can be Whole.

The Soil and the Seed

If my friends were trees
I would live in a forest
And the branches that touch
Bend to bonds long before us

And the vines that entwine
In rhyme beyond time
Are the roots of pursuit
The fruits of their fruit

The essence of friendship
Is Divine delight
Like deified worship
On a Brandywine night

The fourth quarter rises
And the Son is in sight
And His water supply is
Our God given right

It quenches the thirst
Of all of our need
It's the last and the first
It's the Soil and the Seed.

This Oven of Clay

There's nothing as loud
As the sound when we pray
There's no path to follow
When you lead the way
There's nothing as warm
As the bread of today
Baked in the body
This oven of clay

There is no greater presence
Than the absence of doubt
The kingdom's within
And within is without
The judgement of others
What's that all about
You have to go in
If you want to get out

We rise to the substance
As though we are yeast
The light feeds us all
From the west to the east
With wisdom that's buried
But never deceased
Come, be born again
Come, be released

There's no place like home
And home I shall say
Is where we belong
But not where we stay
For as Light we expand
We are all on our way
To already there
In this oven of clay.

Eve Returning

As fireflies flash the Light of Soul
Expressing midnight to the Moon
I fly by on dreams of Venus
After transiting in June

Awake now to the Feminine
Dancing down upon the Earth
In soothing shades and shadows
Announcing Wisdom and Rebirth

For Eve once held in Adam
Was freed to take the Fall
Time is now for the return
Of Her place within us All.

All That Ever Mattered

We are One
We must proclaim this
Though our voices may be scattered
It is this
That brings us Love
And Love is all that ever mattered

The depth of desire
That demands our attention
Is the tip of temptation
The spark of ignition

No matter for what you are searching
There is more that lay undiscovered
For in finding oneself we find others
And all of God becomes uncovered

There is no us, there only Is
One cannot become undone

There exists a solitary beautiful Birth
From which we all have come

But our roots are now spread widely
Twisting paths to Kingdom Come
Yet the Truth of our existence
Is the same for everyone

But duality has shattered souls
Taken reason for a ride
In order to return for reunion
One must literally step outside

So we feel we are separate
Removed from whence we came
Fact is we never left
Just started living in the brain

And reason, once again,
Slithers in with sweet disdain
To be the coil of turmoil
Seeming sane inside insane

Free is the Mansion in which One lives
With many rooms and not one fence
Let go this sense of being
Of being any part of sense

We are One
We must proclaim this
Though our voices may be scattered
It is this
That brings us Love
And Love is all that ever mattered.

Godspeed

And as I cleared the seventh hill
My eyes were blessed with
The vision of seven more
My legs, not a moment before
So tired and so in belief
They were nearing their summit
Became alive again with
A spirit to run
But first . . .
I dance
Dance with all the
Spirits that live within
Each and every blade of grass
My support, my bed, my food
The sky beneath my feet
Opens me to the land above my head
When Glory be the propellant
Of the mission

Grace moves faster than
The speed of Light
This is known as
Godspeed.

Acclimation (Dancing with Mr. DNA)

It is powerful to fall apart
What is even more powerful
Is when the pieces you fall apart into
Begin to fall apart

There is a physical reward
For a mental breakdown

Your Being becomes more alive

You become stronger on a cellular level
Millions of muscles that lay dormant in denial
Are now activated by acclimation
They recognize their strength
In a universal connection

To universal perfection
They release any attachment to separation
They bond with particles of Grace
That have orbited them since Birth

Awaiting their Ascension

Their re-establishment in Truth
Which in truth
Was in their establishment
There never was a separation to reunite into
Only an awakening to live not only in light
But in the majesty of darkness as well

I am not separate from the demons
That dance in my DNA
But the demons that dance in my DNA
Appear to separate me from myself

I accept this no more

I choose now a new partner
One who has been dancing in my shoes
All along.

Mind of the Master

When I bathe in God's love
My thoughts become clean
They bristle with Grace
And burst at the seam

My imaginings have no context
For I've never dreamt this extreme
Yet I know that it is the Truth
Because it's so simple and serene

No confusion about the illusion
I am perfect and pristine
I'm in the Mind of the Master who made me
That Master's Mind now as me can be seen.

And Became

We awaken to the Infinite Power
Of our Energy
As we Become
In tune
With the way it is exchanged

There is no Separation
Between Giving and Receiving

The Art of Giving
Contains
The Reward of Receiving

They are One

And one cannot Receive oneself
Without Giving oneself

Only in Giving can we Become
And Becoming awakens our Giving

We Become our own Reward
When we Give of Ourselves

I know because:

I gave up Judgement
And found Beauty

I gave up Expectation
And received Beauty

I gave up Myself
And Became Beauty.

Arise

Do you languish in the morning
Like the lilies in the pond
Basking in the waking
Till your senses all respond

Do you linger in the dreams
That sweet release across your night
And bathe inside the warmth
That washes you as light

Can you feel my thoughts from miles
As they touch you deep as breath
Can you sense me in your cells
Strong as life, brave as death

We have risen to the moment
Through our desire just to be
And the stars aligned to find us
Amongst this vast infinity

For desire frees our freedom
Through the love we love to make
It is the waking of our Being
To our being wide awake.

Rain as Reign (My Thirst Is My Worship)

What a wonderfully wet way
To slide into the day
Dance a little in the cool water
As it splashes on your upturned face
See if you can spot the drop
That will tease your tongue
As it appears above your head
And then laugh aloud
As it splashes
Right upon your nose

We are the Garden
And God waters us to grow

You gonna run and hide
Stay dry and brittle
Or are you gonna
Drink of this blessing
Drown in this Love

I used to see rain as rain
But now I see rain as Reign

My Thirst is my Worship

I swallow drops of wisdom
Little bubbles of My Beloved*

My faith is saturated
And puddles into yours with freedom
Swimming alongside you on the journey
Before we join in the dirt
And grace the Earth with our liquid love

I find now by blessing the plants
I can bless everyone

For by awakening in soil as prayer
I can be the Newtrient
For every soul

May you grow today.

* My acknowledgment and gratitude to Rumi.

The Word

Silence is the sound
Of so many things
Like a flower blooming
Or the flutter of wings

Silence is the sound
Of holding hands
As well as the mysteries
No one understands

Silence is the sound
In the ring of a tree
Silence is the sound
That is deep within me

Silence is the blue
Of water reflecting
Silence is the sound
Of Jesus resurrecting

Silence is truth
And truth shall abound
Silence is the place
Where God is found

Silence is a scream
That cannot be heard
Until ears are lost
And there is only
The Word.

The Eyes of God

I extended the thought
Of my hand
And became the touch
That Michelangelo painted

I not only graced
My etheric fingers
Through the hair of God
I became alive within each root

I am an outgrowth
From the source
Of all Love

I wave in the wind
From the breath
Of life given

And I spread that essence
Through my every action

My soul is on a mission to find
All my Brothers and Sisters
And caress them with
The wisdom of laughter

Till we all are smiles
Gleaming in the eyes of God.

Answers in the Ashes

Some things must be burned
For others to be built
Our lives flow like water
But our lessons come like silt

Where we are is more important
Than anywhere that we can go
What we give gives us power
And awakens us to Flow

To be in the breath I take
Is to ring within the tree
For to be inside myself
I must first grow out of me

It is between where we begin
To understand that we are One
And for all I've yet to do
There is more that I have done

I carry in my vessel
All the light I'll ever need
I am oak to the acorn
And God the soil to my seed

When I am flame to the fire
Then to burn becomes my task
For there are answers in the ashes
Beyond what questions can ever ask.

Tears of the Soul

Many of us never let anyone go deep enough to
hurt our soul
But down there
Deep in there
Lay the abyss of assimilation
The scattered insufficiencies
That litter about what we call garbage
Garbage is glorious
For what we throw away
Is what we find too sacred to save
Conditions that can heal themselves
Let it be
Leave it alone
Bullshit!
We must dive into the deluge
Disappear into the divinity of denial
The refuse of religion
The pain of a soul

Growing in each life
With each breath
Closer to God
Yet farther from faith
For it is God
I have scattered into a division of
Acceptance for all
Or idiosyncrasies of indecision

Every mistake is only a perceptual challenge.

A removal of participation
For one of observance
Can distance our delicate egos
From the self judgement that ensues
When we hurt
And even more so
When we feel we have hurt others
How do I know everything is perfect
Because it's happening
And countless joys have come in eventualities
To teach me this
And more
But tears from my soul
Opened me to the wisdom
That lay in my shadow
The stuff I hid in the Light.

By excavating the denied me
I uncovered the Divine me

For Divinity is not only Divine
It is more than that
It is the pain, anger, hurt and judgment
That we say we don't do
It is in that denial
Where the tears of my soul
Have fallen to water my heart
Into growth where I didn't even know I had soil
Denial itself
Has rooted my acceptance
And I Grow
I Expand
I Open

And not just to the rosy parts
Or the insanely sensuous parts
Or the incredible energetic communicative parts
No . . .
These are the glorious
God given highs of love
But in the depth of love
The fractured buried basements
That things eventually seep out of
That's where love opens its true splendour
Its commitment to us eternally

Until we accept All of us
Every twisted truth and lascivious lie

I have never been more complete
Than Right Here
Right Now

As tears from my soul
Wash the sacred water of the Divine
Into barren oceans that have thirsted evermore
From each tortured time I have stated
I am NOT
I am NOT
Once again
Bullshit
I Am

I am everything I love about love
I am also everything I despise about love
I cannot fully become alive in love
Until I accept that I am the death of love as well
I am all of this
And my Soul knows
For it has shown me its glory
Now
It shows me its pain

I accept that my soul hurts
And I am in pain

And in knowing this
I have become more
More caring
More daring
Complete
Whole

Tears of my soul
One of the most painful
Sad events
I have ever experienced

Tears of my soul
They are what washes me
Closer to my truth

My denial of my own acceptance
Has brought me acceptance of my own denial
The beauty of this may look really warped
In this reality
Yet it is perfect
On all levels
In all dimensions
Or it would not be happening

The deep tears of my soul
Have put soul deep in my tears

And I drown as I breathe
I laugh as I cry
I flower as I root
I rise in love
I fall in love
I am a rainbow of black and white
Shades of redemption for shadows of revelation
Vibrating high
Vibrating low
Any vibration affects all vibration

I am only half alive in my joy
I awaken the other half in my tears

These little drops of wisdom
That grace our cheeks
Are also the mist of a mysterious Divinity
That not only cries with us
She cries within us

If I am truly to believe that I am All that I am
Then I must include All that I believe I am not.

Loss as Prophet

Death is something only the living
Have to deal with
Those who've passed are busy being reborn
As the morning dew on fertile flowers
That grace our souls with the renaissance of smell
Some are just too beautiful to be confined to a body
They are meant to be shared
They are among the mist that makes the clouds
For to rain upon us purely peace
They are in the very air that we breathe
And each breath
Each and every breath
Divine
They moved us through their existence
Now their existence moves through us
Because they shared with us a life of love
We now live our lives with love to share.

Becoming a Saint

I found myself
In the rings of a tree
A black walnut one
That called to me

In a voice that splintered
The echoes of time
This tree spoke to my Spirit
In eternal rhyme

From a sturdy branch
I grew as a leaf
That reached to the Sun
As Love to Belief

I taste the soil
As it feeds my Soul
And I flower in the power
Of an unseen control

For there are limits to life
As we know it to be
But free is the growth
That made me a tree

I am born with each breath
As a seed to be sown
And I live because dying
Allows me to roam

I am the center of the cross
I am that intersection
I am what I am
Through eternal resurrection

Part Spirit, part human
Part what is and what ain't
I'm a fallen Angel
Becoming a Saint.

Completely Incomplete

The absolute purity of Truth
Lies between each breath

When we are neither breathing in
Nor breathing out

We are the stillness of the seventh day
When even the Creator took a break

We are the potential of a chance
The epitome of yet to be

We are the lotus unopened

We are birth in all its glory
Without ever being born

Empowered with closure
Before the beginning

Seeded and fertilized

An egg before the shell

An eternal idea
Borne of One Love

An expected passion

With no connection to a state of being
For we have yet to become

We are the stars in the sky
Before there was a sky

We are the thought of a Shiva
Before she was even dust

We are the essence of a savior
Before one was ever needed

Consumed in the purity of peace
Swallowed in the belly of beyond before

Giving in is not giving up

Surrender is acceptance, not defeat

Understanding this means nothing
And nothing exists by itself

Nothing is the space between breaths
Find yourself in space

All of It

We are Complete
Long before
We are Incomplete.

A Cocoon of Possibility

The first kiss echoed of reincarnation
I could taste my past on her lips
She was a part of me
Before I was

Like a fingerprint
In the womb

Her tongue could unleash
My soul
And her eyes
Comfort my destiny

She made me question my reality
By answering my will

I saw her as a shadow once
With my eyes twice removed
She was close to being
Distantly inside me

A cocoon of possibility
Where even butterflies are entranced

We know not our full beauty
Till it is opened by another

For though my wings
May carry wonder
It is the wind that
Fuels their flight

She is the breeze
That rebirthed me
From my jar of clay

She is the dream
I dreamt into being
From the dust of dawn
Within her dream

The sculpture . . . rethought
The sculptor . . . reborn

The artist becomes the art
And the union is complete

Now
We Create.

Ribbons

I looked at what appeared
To be a blank sheet of paper
And saw letters dangling above
Like strings from time unwinding
They spun and bounced
And laughed among themselves
And as I waved my hand into them
They gathered on my fingers
In an order of unexpected precision
But anticipated connection
As if I could make any word
At any time
And it would speak in sense
In one or several dimensions

I did not even have to know
Their meaning
They knew
And entranced through me

And in trance
I welcomed them to form
Writing, as it were
Like pyramids on sand

I was the support
for their foundation
But I was constantly shifting

How could I write
Outside myself
What was beyond words
Inside of me

I couldn't
But they could

The dancing letters
The drops of thought
The spatial paradigms
They knew how to bypass my filters
Overlook my own observations
And couch together
In sinewy ribbons of elegance
That turn my fingers into
Wands of enlightenment

I pour wisdom through my pen
Because I am wise enough
To get out of the way

Once

I was Poet

Now

I have become the Poem.

Jehovah of Hoshea

After bathing in the brilliance of night
I welcome the morning of my dawning
I, one of many wonders,
Am experiencing an explosion
Into a new consciousness

On a larger level
I am the Spirit
Flowing through the Spirit
That is flowing through me

I am inside of the Cells
that are inside of Me

I am the Walk
Of my own Stillness

I am not only Love
I am the Whisper
Inside of Love

The Sap that Caresses
The Growth of a Tree

The Impossible Pressure
That Diamond's Coal

The Lift of Flight

The Grace of Resurrection

The stone was not rolled away
for an exit

It was Moved for
Our Perception
Of Glory.

The Purpose of Me

I am attached to nothing
Yet love and honor everything

I am written in peace
Yet still have bindings of war

I am alive in every moment
Yet dying every second

I am lost within the light
Yet find myself in darkness

I am given to extremes
Yet taken so simply

I am One with the Lord
Yet twice I became

I am seeking union
By dividing time

I am complete in pieces
That form my whole

I am finding in living
That living means finding

The purpose of me
In questioning myself.

A wise spirit once said,

"A flower is the visual interpretation
of the plant's enlightenment."

As the plant reaches perfect union
With its own unique Glory
It blossoms into
An expression of Love

It reaches for God and succeeds

It is One with the Light
It bathes in the wonder
And releases the scent
Of Heaven
On Earth

It attracts everything to it
Then Gracefully dies
To nourish
Its Self.

I Heard God Laughing

I fell asleep inside a dream
And dreamt I was awake
Walking upon clouds
That floated on a lake

And as I peered above
I saw the ground below
And realized all I knew
Were just things I thought were so

And then my wings expanded
Into rainbows made of light
And I arched into the darkness
And dayed the deepest night

And then I heard God laughing
And the sound was that of breath
And it woke into me life
And life awoke inside my death.

The Water in the Well

The water in the well
Is deeper than blue

The water in the well
Is what makes me in you

The water in the well
Is drawn with intent

The water in the well
Knows what is meant

The water in the well
Is a chalice for change

The water in the well
Is arranged to rearrange

The water in the well
Is not to quench a given thirst

The water in the well
Will everlast any first

The water in the well
Is not water that you drink

The water in the well
Is a way in which to think.

Deep Inside of You

It lay inside in comfort
Waiting to be shared
It wants to ride the forefront
Only pure when it is bared

To flow inside the movement
Spill its grace on every beach
Making light the heavy phases
That weigh the steps we take to reach

The essence that lay buried
In each and every thing we do
It sculpts the clay we call ourselves
And puts me deep inside of you

For it is passion that I speak of
And in all it has to be
For to live our lives without it
Is to never really see

The bristles of the brush
That paint the sky before the dawn
Or the hand that weaves its wonder
Upon our soul when we are born

We can work and play and drift away
To corners far beyond our dreams
We can fly so high with passion
That oftentimes it seems

It is this alone that matters
For without it what could be
It sculpts the clay we call ourselves
And puts you deep inside of me

For it is passion that has made us
So it is passion we shall give
We will find its strength together
And it will teach us how to live.

Mandara:
From Petals to Priestess

Her name itself
Sprinkles upon
The tongue
Like the droplets
That nourish
Her spirit

She is the flower
Dangling from
Buddha's finger
Swinging in Grace
That blooms
From her breath

She speaks in waves
Liquid love

That rolls
Seashells
Upon the sands
Of Heaven

She is
Beach
To beauty
And she
Skies
In blue

Her eyes caress
The very windows
Of wisdom
She is
Expectation
Awakened

Peering at
Love from
Inside and Out
For she
Is flower
To the stem
Of my possibility

She is
Mandara
Buddha's beloved
The blossom
Of His Being

She has become
My friend
And I
I have become
More.

Shimshai

I went to hear him as I,
But when I left
I was not

The strings of my being
Were upon his guitar

I was touched by the talons
Of eagles
Masquerading as the fingers
Of angels

I was no longer
I became the moment

Swirling into others like spilled paint

A yin of every color
For a yang so black and white

Balance takes two
Until balanced

Then we are All with the One
For we are One with the All.

Rookery

Feathers are the manifestation
Of the flight of Spirit

A brush upon Nature's breeze
That softly paints our destinies
A visual sense that caresses our eyes
And dusts our skin
With the colors of
Love's effervescence

Perceived by some as Aura
And by others
Oblivious in oblivion
Invisible

Nevertheless
When one is awakened
All are enlightened

Pay attention
Find the elation vibration
Be aware
To the calling
To the message
For the message is sent
In such myriad ways

And each Word part of the Breath
That Gospels our Glory

We speak into Nature
Our own being

We are the light captured
In the Himalayan honey
Hanging from the majesty
Of the mountainside
Buzzed by the brilliance
Of a million little wings
Creating a cool wind
That massages the passing clouds

Great pillows of Love

Where eagles fly on freedom
That whispers of Heaven

Their feathers scented by the musk
Of petite deer
Who prance to impress a mate

And the scent rises to grace
The air that hangs in droplets of life
Drifting down delicately and tenderly
Upon the highest rookery on Earth
And dusts the newborn feathers
With love
So close
To truth
It melts
The heart
Of the mountain

And she cries in rivers
That nourish us all
And she evaporates
And radiates
And disappears
Into the air

Then dusts our skin
In the Flow

In the Flow of the Ohm

In the Flow of the One

Who spoke us
Into Being.

Thirty Lashes Away

The slither is silent
When the serpent is sacred

The essence of perception
When altered and accepted
Is to bow within the reptile
As if you never self-erected

Are you scared
Of your own power
Are you in the second
Or in the hour
Are you here in full avail
For the power that shall unveil
Are you one who sees the light
Have you awakened pure and bright

Under a star
Above a manger
In the straw
Without stranger

Do you know the Child of God
The Holy Spirit deep within
Do you know that to be saved
You must first be lost in sin

For to return is why we left
Or rather, separated from the Source
And now we are the magnet matter
That draws design and charts a course

To a place of symbiosis
A Place of Caring, Warmth, and One
Where we become what Love allows
And Love allows us to become.

Cannes Brulles

Whispers like dust
fell between the spaces in the lines I wrote
It seemed easy to sweep his memory
Into the suggestion of words

Not until we bathed in the sweet haunt of tears
That fell like Spanish moss over the shoulders
We shared
Did I realize my father truly loved me
Each tear illuminating the memory of a young boy
Whose every dream trickled off his fingers
Into the tiny hand he held

I was the innocence in his guilt
And the forgiveness of his faults

He cut a piece of cane and fed me
The natural sugar it held
It was at that moment that he exposed me

To the Love within
But it was up to me to go inside

I remember that day
And I remember very well
Mixing with the sweet smell
From the fields of Cannes Brullee

He was more of a gypsy than a father
And he was perfect for me
All I ever needed was given to me
When I held his hand

He walked in and out of my life
And woven in the wonder of his sporadic appearing
He taught me
Or more precisely
He awakened in me
How to cherish each and every taste
No matter how long between each sip

For in between gives depth
To once in a while
And once in a while
Gives space to depth

No one ever really leaves anyone
They just find us in someone else.

The Caged Divine

I surrendered to the aura
And her wings I saw so clear
I washed my hands, she washed my soul
And draped a whisper cross my ear

I will share with you the morning's dew
We shall wear it as a cloak
We'll bathe our spirit in vibration
Till we're the incense of our smoke

I find it is less about me making love
And more about love making me
The complete symbiosis of bodies in bliss
Can reveal and heal what I feel is amiss

I glimpse the Now in the Everafter
My orgasms come with laughter
Then tears spill like well aged wine
Letting go free . . . The Caged Divine.

Reliquary

Sunshine scattered through the lazy afternoon
It was the fifth Sunday in the fifth month of 2011
Energies were syncing
Spirits were raising
Before this day had wandered out of night
The Moon had reached its apogee
The place where it is furthest from the Earth
It was also neither waxing nor waning
It was at that millisecond

That twinkling of an I

From one to the other

When emptying becomes filling
When releasing becomes accepting
When letting go becomes letting in
It was transition

True transition
From one to the other
Yet always in tune
I had no idea how personal
The Moon had been with me earlier
For I was about to transition
And if I had known to what extent
I would've eaten something first

There are fortunes that find us
When we listen with our souls

My path had brought me a session
With a Shamanic Healer
And as I lay upon the table
And gently closed my eyes
I was re-born
No, un-born

A primal Soul

I became the Heart at the Center of Aum
The Center that has no Center
The Sound that made Sound
The Vibration of Love

The way God speaks to God

She made sounds that I'd never heard before
At least none I'd heard for the last seven
Lifetimes or so
Sounds of impossible origins, but familiar places
Sounds that painted caves long before we did
Sounds that danced the sky and rippled the water
Sounds that were beyond within and above without
Sounds that were laid as fine as mist upon me
And as deep as roots into me
As if I were an altar

A reliquary

I was the bush not consumed by the flame
I felt feathers where there once were thorns
I felt flight was possible
Shit, not only possible, it was happening

She caressed me in tongues that knew no words

For that is how the Soul hears
And I heard Truth

This empowered my wings to expand
And beat with the rhythm of All that is One
For a while I could fly
Like a wave of sound

And then I became the sky

The sounds that chose to come through her
Were the resonance of the Ancients
The Keepers that disappear
If we listen too hard
They are only seen in absence
And only felt in passing
They have the presence of an echo
When you don't hear the initial sound

They are channeled vibrations of source
The tune in the tuning forks
Nature expressed in audible silence
As tones and waves within us
She channeled in vibration and color
A myriad of tones that all came from the One
I was saturated in a bath of Spirit
I was in love

I was Love

I was the sound that formed Sound
The Sound of the Light
I saw what I was hearing
Like I was hearing with my eyes
And I was feeling with my ears
As if they could touch the vibration
I could feel the temperature

And sense the texture
Of each and every ripple
From each and every wave
It was sanctity awakening
And it swallowed my absolvement

She had opened a portal
That stirred digestion of the Truth within me
My third chakra rumbled in its yellow light
Then exploded into a green star
That spread me like space

Like space on fire

Sparkling and blazing in my rainbow of changes

A Cosmic Chameleon

Completely and eternally alive in the Sound

In the Word

I am this perpetual resonation
I am the Sound before the Sound

I am the True Reliquary

For I am a Home to God's Breath
And I am a House for Her Glory.

About the Author

Michael Murphy Burke was born in New Orleans, Louisiana, on September 30, 1959. This happens to be the same day that Rumi, the great Sufi mystic poet, was born. This is not a coincidence, as "coincidence is just God's way of staying anonymous."

Michael grew up surrounded by music, art, passion, freedom of expression, and the absolute power of living on his own path. He's been a poet all his life, with his first published material being in his high school newspaper when he was a sophomore. More recently, he contributes steadily to *Oracle Magazine* and is also published in *Aquarius Magazine* and *Conscious Life Journal.*

In addition to writing, Michael also creates artistic visions in a variety of woods for private clients as a custom woodworker. He can also be found doing spoken word and sacred sound shows and meditations throughout the Atlanta area and beyond as a sound artist.

The Enclosed CD Includes:

Awaken to the aural landscapes of ambient architecture through these five spoken-word selections set to various instrumentation and effects on this limited CD.

TRACKS
1. The Echo of Light
2. One Can Only
3. Reliquary
4. Cause for Another
5. The First Taste of a Feast

The poems for tracks 1, 2, and 3 can be found in this book.

Tracks 4 and 5 are unique to this limited CD.

Please enjoy the audiobook of *Dancing with the Divine* at michaelmurphyburke.com.